Stuart F. Weld

The Eastern Question and a Suppressed Chapter of History

Napoleon III and the Kingdom of Roumania

Stuart F. Weld

The Eastern Question and a Suppressed Chapter of History
Napoleon III and the Kingdom of Roumania

ISBN/EAN: 9783337246259

Printed in Europe, USA, Canada, Australia, Japan

Cover: Foto ©ninafisch / pixelio.de

More available books at **www.hansebooks.com**

THE EASTERN QUESTION

AND A SUPPRESSED CHAPTER OF HISTORY

NAPOLEON III.

AND THE

KINGDOM OF ROUMANIA

BY

STUART F. WELD

WITH AN INTRODUCTION

BY REV. EDWARD EVERETT HALE, D.D.

"A forgotten, or, indeed, almost a suppressed chapter of history."— JOHN FISKE

BOSTON
GEO. H. ELLIS, 141 FRANKLIN STREET
1897

Mr. Weld has devoted much time and study to unveiling the mysteries which have surrounded the creation of Roumania, and which have attended Eastern diplomacy in all the recent history of that State. Mr. Weld has found, as any student finds who attempts the difficult studies attending the history of the Second Empire, that the part taken by Napoleon III. in the making of that history has been construed in different ways according as men hated Napoleon or as they flattered him. As one of his French authorities says, "Napoleon's history has passed through the double criticism of hate and love." From sources not largely studied, even in Europe,— not studied at all, one might say, in America,— Mr. Weld has constructed an intelligible history of the diplomacy, the intrigue, the failures, and final success which have attended the history of Roumania since that name was given to the provinces which were united in the new-born kingdom. As has been aptly remarked by Professor John Fiske in reference to this study, Mr. Weld has reproduced a lost passage in history.

It will be seen that at the meeting at Osborne, in 1857, of the sovereigns of France and of England, a meeting interesting at the time, and celebrated since, the first important step was taken which led forward to the establishment of the new kingdom. Prince Albert, however, opposed any immediate action; and the plan of Napoleon III. was for the moment delayed. The determination of the people of Wallachia was strongly in favor of such union. The people of Moldavia, if they wanted it, were not at first permitted to express themselves. But not long after the Osborne incident the legislature of Moldavia, by a vote of eighty-one to two, expressed the almost unanimous wish of that province for union. For a considerable time, however, the wish of the people of the two provinces was thwarted by the opposition of England and Austria. A motion introduced by Mr. Gladstone, then in opposition, favoring the union, was defeated in Parliament. All the same, however, the people of the two provinces themselves went forward to carry out their own purposes. By an extraordinary movement of popular enthusiasm, Moldavia and Wallachia, each having the privilege to choose its hospodar, chose the same person, Colonel Couza. He was chosen Prince of Moldavia in January, Prince of Wallachia in February, 1859. Here was practical union; and Napoleon, in his address to the French Chambers, February 7, said with some pride, "If I were asked what interest France has in these countries, I should answer that the interest of France is everywhere where a cause of justice and civilization is to be maintained."

Mr. Weld's history, which is in the reader's hands, shows how very close was Napoleon's connection with the subsequent events which his policy, indeed, up to this time had foreseen and prepared the way for.

The tendency of the last half of the present century has been to union. United Italy and United Germany are illustrations of this tendency on the continent of Europe. The increasing commerce of the States of America, the virtual establishment of the Monroe Doctrine, and the great Pan-American Congress are the most signal illustrations of the same determination in this country. Illustrations on a smaller scale, but not less interesting, are those of the establishment of the States on the Danube, which give to Europe and civilization a new barrier against the barbarism of the crowned assassin of Stamboul. Mr. Weld's study of the history of Roumania will open the eyes of most American readers to the difficulties which ancient diplomacy and the conservative prejudices of half Europe have placed in the way of such consolidation of States. All the more interesting is a history of one of the great providential movements in which is answered that prayer which foreshadows the Christian civilization of the future.

That prayer was answered in a certain measure in the Constitution of the United States, which made one nation out of many. It was answered when the Italian provinces formed themselves into the Kingdom of Italy; when the petty duchies of Germany united with such kingdoms as Bavaria and Prussia in the formation of the Empire of Germany; when Austrians and Hungarians consent to the dual Empire of Austria; and when the kingdom of Roumania came into being in the face of jealousies and of the sway of ancient prejudices.

Civilization advances and the kingdom of heaven comes as children of God work together with him to bring about the hope and the prayer of the Saviour of mankind,—

" That they all may be one."

EDWARD E. HALE.

THE EASTERN QUESTION AND A SUP-PRESSED CHAPTER OF HISTORY.

NAPOLEON III. AND THE KINGDOM OF ROUMANIA.

Our historian George Bancroft wrote in 1867 : " It is the glory of the French nation that it has, on many decisive occasions, put forth its strength on the side of liberty ; and the Netherlands, the United States, and Italy bear witness to her effective services as the defender of nationalities and the soldier of freedom."

No instance better illustrates these words than that furnished by France, Roumania, and the Crimean War. Not one man in a thousand, however, is aware of the services of France in this case, still less of the fact that the prime, successful mover was Napoleon III.

No doubt the estimate of this remarkable ruler has, since his fall in 1870, lost some of the harshness which then characterized it. A French writer, M. de La Gorce, has just published the third volume of his " History of the Second Empire," bringing the work down to 1861. The preface begins as follows : —

" The reign of Napoleon III. has been judged thus far either through favor or hatred. Twice it has undergone the test of falsehood,— the falsehood of adulation during its time of power, the falsehood of calumny when the time of misfortune came. To this reign, brilliant and inauspicious, superficial and tragic, I propose to apply the customary rules of criticism, which establish facts according to testimony, and thus restore to their true places men and events."

No better purpose could be entertained. This is scarcely the place, however, to discuss how far our author has succeeded. When we find a passage like the following, we are ready to ask whether M. de La Gorce is not fighting vigorously the "falsehood of calumny" of which he speaks. Of Napoleon III. he says: "He had the ambition to re-establish the liberty which he had formerly overthrown. Above all, he loved the people, not his own people especially (for he was more of a humanitarian than a patriot), but all peoples; that is to say, the poor, the weak, the disinherited." When, upon another page, we read that the *coup d'état* was "one of the greatest crimes against society which any ruler of any civilized nation has committed during the present century," we are tempted to ask whether our author's estimate differs, after all, from the estimates of Kinglake and Victor Hugo. With regard to the *coup d'état*, nevertheless, he states circumstances which, he avers, gave some sort of justification to the act.

To show the way in which our writer compounds praise and blame so as to challenge the reader, it would seem, to draw his own conclusions, we add the following: De La Gorce describes Napoleon as having qualities not common, adding, however, that he possessed everything which makes a sovereign unfortunate; that is, high purposes without the wisdom to carry them out. In spite of this, let us remember to what extent Napoleon did carry out his high purposes, among which are to be reckoned the liberation of Italy and the liberation of Roumania. Henri Martin, the Republican historian, says in like manner, in his "Popular History of France" (vol. iii. p. 538): "His character was a complex one. He had great aims, but he failed in their realization."

We quote again: "When face to face with public calamities and in the midst of conspiracies, he displayed a calm and simple courage *qui conquit même ses adversaires.*"

A final sketch of the historian's plan is found in the following : —

"One personage dominates this entire history,— the mysterious man who during eighteen years incarnated in himself the life of the nation. At the origin of his career, when he baffled with equal dexterity the plots of demagogues and intrigues of parliamentarians, it was the fashion to laugh at his incapacity. When his throne had been established by violence and consecrated by popular suffrage, so much good fortune dazzled, not only vulgar minds, which bow down to success, but also *les esprits élevés qui osent discuter les arrêts de la fortune*. Finally, misfortunes came, so bitter that all reprobation is lost in one immense compassion."

It may be added that the work of M. de La Gorce has been crowned by the French Academy,— a distinction which it certainly deserves.

In one of the extracts furnished, our author refers to Napoleon III. as a "mysterious man." It is precisely because, in spite of the researches of De La Gorce, so much mystery still attaches to Napoleon and so much need exists of further research that the present sketch has been written.

An element aside from that which relates to the "mysterious man" points to the examination suggested.

At a time when the Armenian massacres and the Greek war have attracted attention to the famous Eastern Question, and some have imagined that the time of its solution was near, it may be well to consider an element of the problem not yet examined. The origin of the Kingdom of Roumania and the part taken by Napoleon III. constitute this element. In 1831 Mazzini predicted that the Question of Nationalities, or Principle of Nationality, would give its name to our century; and there is reason to believe that this principle is to be carried out to a great extent in the settlement of the Eastern Question. The Principle of Nationality was the basis of the policy adopted by Napoleon and his government. The facts to be narrated are so little known that we have ventured to refer to them as a suppressed, or we might say neglected, chapter of history.

Let us inquire what this suppressed chapter was.

Few persons are aware of the fact referred to in the following telegrams. A despatch to the London *Times*, dated Bucharest, Jan. 15, 1873, said: "Funeral services in honor of the Emperor Napoleon will be held in all the churches in the country to-day. The entire Roumanian press contains sympathetic obituary notices of the deceased emperor."

A despatch from Bucharest to the Bonapartist paper, *L'Ordre*, said: "To-day a funeral service for Napoleon occurred throughout the country. The journals publish obituaries and express sentiments of sympathy."

The following telegram to the London *Times* does not refer to the funeral services, but its import is similar to that of the above despatches. It is dated Bucharest, Jan. 24, 1873. "The Chamber of Deputies to-day unanimously voted an address of condolence with the Empress Eugénie."

The celebration of these rites would have had less significance if at the time of his death Napoleon had been emperor. Save in two States — Italy and Roumania — scant honor was shown his memory. It is not the way of the world to pay respect to the fallen, and the fact that in these States it was paid to Napoleon redounds both to their honor and his. Still, this action was not perhaps what one might expect.

Neither would one suspect Prince Charles of Roumania, a Hohenzollern, of undue anxiety to honor a Bonaparte. Indeed, one special consideration might have influenced him against such a manifestation. The candidature of his brother, Prince Leopold, to the Spanish throne had precipitated the war of 1870; and it was owing to the persistence of Napoleon III. in requiring the withdrawal of this candidature that Prince Leopold retired. But, if Prince Charles knew that Napoleon had prevented his brother from acquiring the Spanish crown, he might have asked himself to what extent he was indebted to the emperor for his own. He heartily united in the wish of the people of Roumania to honor Napoleon. What Napoleon effected in behalf of Roumania is referred to briefly or not at all in the histories of the time ; and almost the same may be said respecting his American and English biographies, although the British work occupies four volumes.* .

It is easier to ask why these events have been neglected than to give a satisfactory explanation. As a reply in part, however, it may be conjectured that events in those half-civilized, if not half-barbarous, provinces of Turkey, could not be expected to attract so much attention as events elsewhere. Few had sagacity enough to perceive the meaning of the changes which successively occurred. Besides, neither the present Republican government of France nor Republican writers have shown much zeal in recognizing or putting on record the acts of the Second Empire which merit praise. But there is a further explanation. During the year subsequent to the Treaty of Paris, Napoleon and the czar had an interview at Stuttgard ; and a *rapprochement* between France and Russia — powers which had been so recently at war — was effected. From that time to the present, if we except the date of the last Polish revolt, 1863, friendly sentiments have existed between France and the Muscovite Empire. In 1893 and 1896 the understanding between these States reached a climax during the demonstrations which attended the visit of the Russian fleet to France and the visit of the czar to Paris. French authors, whatever their party preferences, have seemed reluctant to discuss or even state the " true inwardness " of

---

* The British biographer, Blanchard Jerrold, relates in detail the circumstances of Napoleon's visit to Osborne in 1857. The facts so closely concerned the British government that they could scarcely escape the notice of a British writer.

the Crimean War. How Napoleon III. thwarted Russia, how he established upon her southern border a compact and progressive State,— these things have been passed over.

Whatever the reason, the fact is scarcely to be disputed that an entire chapter — *that which relates to the origin of the Kingdom of Roumania — has been dropped out of the history of the century.*

While we cannot fail to note the neglect which has fallen upon these events, it is just to observe that an annual publication, the *Annuaire des Deux Mondes,* which has never been accused of Bonapartist proclivities, stated the facts with much fidelity. Six closely printed pages on an average are occupied for twelve years, 1855 to 1866, with a chronicle of Roumanian events, and give an account of the genesis of the kingdom.

Let us review the chief facts connected with the enfranchisement of Roumania and the part of Napoleon. How happened it that Roumania observed those funeral rites Jan. 15, 1873?

Those who read these pages should not imagine that the writer's purpose is to present a summing up of the character and acts of Napoleon III. As M. de La Gorce says, for twenty-five years the empire has suffered from "the falsehood of calumny." The evils of this period have been pointed out and multiplied. Our plan is to show in part the reverse of the picture. The achievements of the emperor should be considered as well as his blunders and faults. Then alone can a verdict be rendered. It is especially our design to examine one of Napoleon's great achievements which has been in a remarkable manner ignored,— the liberation of Roumania.

First of all, let us call to mind that the origin of the Kingdom of Roumania is intimately connected with the Eastern Question, one of the greatest questions of history. This problem has been of recent years conspicuously before the public because of the anomalous position of

Prince Ferdinand and Bulgaria. To this complication the Armeno-Eastern and Greco-Eastern complication has been added.

On the 26th of March, 1855, when the siege of Sebastopol was half over, Napoleon laid before the powers at the Conference of Vienna the following propositions respecting the Principalities of Moldavia and Wallachia, which form to-day the Kingdom of Roumania: —

First. To unite the Principalities into one.

Second. To confer the sovereignty upon a foreign, not a native, prince.*

Not one of the powers indorsed Napoleon's propositions. But in less than twelve years they were carried out. To what extent did Napoleon contribute toward this result? to what extent did others?

The propositions submitted at Vienna were stated with moderation and reserve. Their shape was almost that of suggestions rather than of formal propositions. Partly on this account and partly because of the prestige which France acquired in the Crimean War, Napoleon was more successful after Sebastopol fell.

March 8, 1856, Count Walewski, the emperor's minister for foreign affairs and president of the Paris Congress, submitted to that body the first of the propositions of 1855. The second was not brought forward. Count Walewski urged the union of the Principalities as a measure in accordance with their interests and with the wishes of the people. This proposal met with less opposition at Paris than at Vienna. France, England, Russia, and Sardinia supported it, while Austria and Turkey continued hostile. As the powers could not agree, the settlement of the question was excluded from the Treaty of Paris and left for later consideration.

But Napoleon had gained a step. In 1855 France alone

* Sixth protocol of the Conference of Vienna. *Annuaire des Deux Mondes* for 1854–55, p. 891.

recommended union. In 1856 union was advocated by four States instead of one.

If, however, the union of the provinces was not effected by the Treaty of Paris, stipulations were inserted which prepared the way for it. The treaty provided that legislatures should be chosen in Wallachia and Moldavia, which should express the preferences of the people as to the organization of the Principalities. These preferences should be submitted to an advisory Commission, to be appointed by the powers. The Commission, having taken into account the votes of the Principalities, should prepare a report and forward it to Paris. Here. the representatives of the powers should be again convoked. The future organization of the Principalities should be decided by them, and their decisions embodied in a convention. Thus the convention known as that of 1858 grew out of the Treaty of 1856. Of that treaty we may regard it as a part.

Another article of the Treaty of Paris strongly favored Moldo-Wallachia.

According to the treaty of Adrianople in 1829, between Russia and Turkey, the privileges which the Principalities enjoyed were confirmed by Turkey and placed under the guarantee of Russia. Virtually, a Russian protectorate was established.* In place of this the Treaty of Paris established a virtual protectorate to be exercised by the signatory powers,— i.e., the five great powers, Sardinia, and the Porte. The privileges possessed by the Principalities were placed under their collective guarantee.

The use which Russia might be expected to make of a Russian protectorate would be, of course, in the interest of Russian aggrandizement. The joint protectorate, however, would naturally be more ready to favor the interest of the Moldo-Wallachian States. But, owing to the ascendency possessed by France and to the interest which Napoleon

*The Turco-Russian Convention of Balta-Liman, concluded in 1849, in some respects strengthened the Russian protectorate.

personally took in the Principalities, the joint protectorate of 1856 was so dominated by France that a sort of French protectorate succeeded the Russian. Accordingly, while the treaty of 1856 did not unite Moldavia and Wallachia, it was one of the helps that prepared the way for union.*

We have seen that Count Walewski laid before the Paris Congress the first of the measures proposed at Vienna (that in favor of the union of the Principalities), and that on this occasion France was supported by England, Russia, and Sardinia. England thus took a liberal position. But her statesmen, influenced by her traditional policy, which had for its basis the integrity of the Ottoman Empire, soon regarded a union of Moldavia and Wallachia as likely to prove a menace to that integrity. England, Austria, and Turkey being once more in accord, England again advocated the anti-union policy which in 1855 had been that of all the powers except France.

The official organ of the French government, the *Moniteur Universel*, made a declaration Feb. 5, 1857, in which the policy of France in favor of the union of the Principalities was reiterated. This led to much discussion in France and England; and no little antagonism of purpose and feeling arose.

Napoleon now determined to make a final effort to secure the co-operation of Great Britain. He proposed that the empress and himself should visit Queen Victoria; and, the offer having been accepted, the sovereigns met at Osborne in the Isle of Wight. Besides the personages named, there were present Prince Albert; Lord Palmerston, the British premier; Lord Clarendon, British ambassador to France; Count Walewski, referred to already; and the Count of Persigny, French ambassador to England.

---

* A further advantage conferred by the treaty of 1856 was the cession by Russia to Moldavia (subject to Turkish suzerainty) of a portion of Bessarabian territory at the mouth of the Danube. At the treaty of Berlin in 1878 Roumania was constrained by the powers to cede this territory back to Russia, accepting a like area of Turkish territory, the Dobrudscha, to the south.

On the morning of August 6 the yacht of the emperor arrived. After breakfast, in the course of a walk, Napoleon and Prince Albert discussed the Roumanian and Eastern Questions. So impressed was the prince by Napoleon's statements that on the day on which their conversation occurred he wrote out a record of it. This "memorandum" occupies six pages in Martin's "Life of the Prince Consort." *

Napoleon argued in favor of the union of the Principalities, Prince Albert against it. In order to show that his policy accorded with the wishes of the people of the provinces, Napoleon related an incident.

The Treaty of Paris had provided for the appointment of an advisory Commission, whose function should be to inquire into the condition of the Principalities. The people of Bucharest were aware of the purposes of France; and, when the French commissioner, Baron Talleyrand, arrived, the populace received him with acclamations, even taking the horses from his carriage and drawing it through the streets.

During the conversation Prince Albert asked Napoleon, "Do you really care for the continuance of the integrity of the Turkish Empire?" The prince observed at the same time that this was a principle which had led England into the French alliance, for which England had made endless sacrifices and which she was determined to maintain with all her energy. Napoleon replied, "If you ask me as a private individual, I do not care for it, and cannot muster up any sympathy for such a sorry set as the Turks. But," he continued, "if you ask me as an *homme politique, c'est une autre chose*. I am of course not prepared to abandon the original object of our alliance, for which France, also, has made great sacrifices." Thus the emperor distinguished between Napoleon the man and Napoleon the *diplomate*. He would not abandon the British alliance. In carrying out the ends of his European policy, this alliance might be of use. But none the less did he adhere to his design to effect a union of the Principalities. This union might eventually prove, *as it did*, inconsistent with the integrity of the sultan's dominions.

Besides the interviews between Napoleon and Prince Albert, others took place between Napoleon and the British and French statesmen already named. But the Englishmen were not to be convinced; and Napoleon was compelled, for the present, to waive his plan of uniting the Principalities. While, however, the emperor could not carry his point, England also made a concession. It referred indirectly to the very point which Napoleon had waived,— the question of union. What was the British concession?

Article 24 of the Treaty of Paris had provided that each Principality should choose a legislative assembly. " These legislatures," the article stated, "shall be called upon to express the wishes of the people with regard to the final organization of the Principalities." Accordingly, the legislatures were chosen. In Wallachia the great majority of the assembly voted for union. In Moldavia the prince, or Hospodar, appointed by the Turkish government, succeeded through frauds and illegalities in getting returned a nominal majority against union. Napoleon urged the sultan to annul these elections, and was joined in his demand by Russia, Prussia, and Sardinia. The Sublime Porte, supported by England and Austria, refused. Finally, France and the protesting powers resorted to coercion, and broke off diplomatic relations with the sultan. Such was the posture of affairs at the time of the visit to Osborne ; and Napoleon insisted, in his conferences with the English statesmen, upon the necessity of rescinding these elections. England finally yielded. On the other hand, as has been said, Napoleon agreed that, in the convention to be concluded, the Principalities should not be united as one State. This was the compromise.

If Napoleon regretted his inability to change the views of

the British government upon the main question, he was gratified by the friendly sentiments entertained by Queen Victoria toward himself and the empress. Writing to her uncle, King Leopold of Belgium, the queen said, "Nothing could be more amiable, kind, pleasant, or *ungênant* than both Majesties were." Respecting the empress, she said, "We are all in love with her, and I wish you knew her." Nor was this the first occasion on which the sovereign of England had expressed herself in like terms. During the last days of the siege of Sebastopol — that siege whose termination liberated, or rather largely contributed toward liberating, Roumania — Queen Victoria, in her diary, Aug. 27, 1855, referred to Napoleon as follows: "I know few people whom I have felt involuntarily more inclined to confide in and speak unreservedly to. I should not fear saying anything to him. I felt — I do not know how to express it — safe with him. . . . There is something fascinating, melancholy, and engaging which draws you to him in spite of any *prévention* you may have against him. . . . He undoubtedly has a most extraordinary power of attaching people to him."

It appears, therefore, that the friendly relations established between the French and English courts in 1855 still continued, although they disagreed upon the question of uniting the Principalities.

As was to be expected, Queen Victoria's views of the Eastern Question agreed with those held by her husband and by Englishmen in general. In her letter to King Leopold, she wrote that the visit of the emperor and empress "was in every way very satisfactory." " Politically," she continues, "it was, as Lord Clarendon said, 'a godsend'; for the unhappy difficulties in the Principalities have been *aplanis* and satisfactorily settled." The good queen meant what she said. But these difficulties were far from settlement. A thin compromise, one not destined to last and which, like the Missouri compromise, did not deserve to last, had been concluded.

On the 10th of August the emperor and empress returned to France. Four days later, August 14, Mr. Gladstone referred in the House of Commons to the Moldavian elections. He said, "It is all very well that these elections should have been quashed; but, if these elections have been a source of jobbery and wicked oppression, why, then, it was to England we ought to have looked to quash them, and that task ought not to have been left to the absolute sovereign of France."

Mr. Gladstone was right. The fact that England defended these elections was not to her honor. In his speech Mr. Gladstone presented a mass of evidence as to the trickery, frauds, and intimidation which had characterized them. England and Austria. finally advised the Porte to cancel them. The new elections resulted, like those in Wallachia, in a great majority for union.

The success thus obtained was followed up. In October, 1857, two months after Napoleon's visit to Victoria, the legislature of Wallachia, by unanimous vote, passed several resolutions, the chief of which repeated the propositions laid before the powers by the emperor in 1855,—those in favor of union and of a foreign prince. In Moldavia, likewise, by a vote practically unanimous (81 to 2), resolutions were passed which comprised these propositions. Few instances have occurred in which a nationality has shown more patriotism, unanimity, and wisdom in the pursuit of its ends.

It was decided that the conference which was to fix the status of Wallachia and Moldavia should meet in Paris in 1858. Mr. Gladstone, who ten years later was to be prime minister of England, was thoroughly in sympathy with the Principalities and with the efforts of France in their behalf, and regretted the attitude of England. On the 4th of May, 1858, before the meeting of the Paris Conference, he moved in the House of Commons that an address be presented to the queen to convey to her majesty the hope of the House that in the negotiations to ensue "just weight may be given to those wishes of the people of Wallachia and of Moldavia which they have recently expressed"; that is, their wish for union.

In his speech, Mr. Gladstone referred to his subject as one "of the utmost interest and importance." The question, he said, "nearly and vitally touches the happiness of millions of our fellow-creatures." "The union of the Principalities," he averred, "is the one great, main, and paramount object of the people by whom they are inhabited." Of the inhabitants, speaking in general, he said: "The people are men attached to the religion which we profess; they are men attached to the liberty which we cherish; they are men who have suffered during a long course of years in consequence of the ambitious policy of aggrandizing neighbors."

In conclusion he said: "France is ready to do her part. She has never departed from her policy. . . . The question whether England shall desert her is a question now to be decided; and the question of that desertion on the one hand, or of perseverance in her policy and redemption of her pledges, is the question which with earnest hope and confidence I this night submit to the House of Commons."

The cheers which greeted these words were not proof that Mr. Gladstone's motion would prevail. His eloquence was recognized by opponents who did not choose to be convinced either by eloquence or facts. Lord Palmerston, the leader of the Liberals, and Disraeli, the leader of the Tories, vehemently opposed Mr. Gladstone. It is amusing now to read their predictions of the evils which would attend a union of the Principalities under a foreign prince,— evils not one of which has come to pass.

The vote stood: for Mr. Gladstone's motion, 114; against it, 292.

If we call to mind that, besides those Liberals who adopted the views of Palmerston, all the Tories voted

against Mr. Gladstone, it appears that the latter carried
with him half or more than half of his party.*

At the close of the debate a strange surprise awaited Mr.
Gladstone. Disraeli, the chancellor of the exchequer, declared that upon this subject there was between the French
and English governments "a perfect identity of sentiment,
of views, and of policy in the widest and truest sense."
Mr. Gladstone scarcely knew what to say. In reply, he observed,— we cannot but note his frankness,—"The right
honorable gentleman has been so enigmatical as to leave
me without the slightest guide for my conduct." The
enigma, however, was quickly solved. The French and
English governments had compromised. Just so they had
compromised at. Osborne. In each case Napoleon had the
advantage. According to the agreement of 1858 the principle of union was, in certain instances, to be introduced
into the convention. To a large extent Napoleon, Gladstone, and the Principalities had their way. As regards
the more ostensible features of the convention, the principle of separation was adopted. Of this compromise Mr.
Gladstone was ignorant. His hope was that the British
government might be brought to give up altogether its opposition to the union of the provinces.

Although Mr. Gladstone's motion was lost, his speech
did much to enlighten public opinion and lessen that dispo-
sition to consult Turkish interests rather than those of
Christians which had marked the policy of Great Britain.
The events which occurred in the Principalities exerted a
like influence.

The debate in the House took place May 4. On May 22
the conference met in Paris under the presidency of Count
Walewski. In opening the debates, he stated that the con-
victions of the French government with regard to the Principalities had been strengthened. To unite Moldavia and
Wallachia as a single State under a foreign prince, his gov-

* At this time the Tories were in power. Lord Derby was premier.

ernment held to be the best solution. Besides, it was a solution which accorded better than any other with the wishes of the people. But he recognized the need of finding a common ground upon which all could stand. On June 5 he presented a plan of convention, and asked that it be accepted as a basis for discussion. This was done. The plan represented, generally speaking, the views of the French and British governments, agreed upon in a spirit of conciliation or — shall we say? — of compromise. Many details had to be discussed, and no less than nineteen sittings of the conference took place. It was not till the 19th of August that the convention was signed. How much union and how much anti-union did this compound contain?

The convention stated that in each Principality the executive functions should be vested in a Hospodar, who should be a native of the Principalities and elected for life. In each the legislative functions were vested jointly in an elective assembly and the Hospodar. But the convention also stated that a Central Commission should be established, which should prepare and submit to each legislature measures of mutual interest to the States. It established a supreme judicial court which was common to both. It stipulated that the organization of the military forces of each Principality should be identical, as though they constituted two corps of the same army. At times these forces were to be united under a single commander. Finally, the official designation of the States was *the United Principalities of Moldavia and Wallachia*. So far as a name goes, this looked more like union than the reverse. One is at once reminded of our national designation, *the United States of America*, as well as that of our kindred beyond the water, *the United Kingdom of Great Britain and Ireland*.

Our attention has thus far been directed exclusively to the question of union. But a reform of another character was effected. Prior to 1858 the government of the sultan had often interfered with the administration and laws of the provinces. By the convention such interference was prohibited, and thus an important step was taken in the direction of autonomy.

As far as it went, the Convention of 1858 was excellent. It had, however, as every compromise has, two aspects. It did not suit the diplomats who had constructed it at Paris. According to some, too little had been done for union; according to others, too much. It did not suit the people of Moldavia and Wallachia. They had no common executive, no common legislature; and it was their purpose to get both.

Here were two States kept apart by the obstinacy of two great Christian powers,— England and Austria,— powers which acted in the interest of Turkey.

They served, of course, their own interests, so far as they understood them. The apprehension of England was that Russia, through the conquest of Turkey and the possession of Constantinople, would become a vast overshadowing power, a peril to Europe and the British possessions in Asia. One question to be decided was as follows,— whether by liberating and strengthening the Christian nationalities of Turkey, *precisely in the way that these objects have been accomplished*, a stronger barrier might not be erected against Russia than through attempts to bolster up the Turk. The latter was the method of England,— that of oppression. The former was the method of Gladstone, Napoleon, and France,— that of freedom.

The fixed purpose of the Principalities was manifest in the action of the new legislatures elected under the Convention of 1858. When the time came to elect in each State an executive, or Hospodar, *the same man was chosen!—* Colonel Alexander Couza. The idea did not at first occur to the members of the Moldavian and Wallachian assemblies that, by choosing the same candidate, the cause of union might be promoted. Colonel Couza, a native of Moldavia, was unanimously chosen by the Moldavian assembly. The Wallachian assembly met shortly after, and several ballots were had; but no candidate received a majority. Then the idea was presented of selecting a candidate already chosen in Moldavia, and Colonel Couza was elected unanimously. Thus did the Principalities circumvent the Convention of 1858, the intent of which did not accord with the double election.

Colonel Couza was chosen Prince of Moldavia Jan. 17, 1859, and Prince of Wallachia February 5. Two days later occurred the opening of the French Chambers. In his address, quoted in part in the Introduction, Napoleon referred to the Principalities and the Convention of 1858 as follows: "The reconstruction of the Danubian Principalities was not effected till many difficulties had been met,—difficulties which interfered with [*qui ont nui à*] the full satisfaction of their most legitimate wishes." "If," he continued, "I were asked what interest France had in these distant countries watered by the Danube, I should answer that the interest of France is everywhere where a cause of justice and civilization is to be maintained."

Exceptions to this chauvinistic statement are found, of course: no exception, however, in the case of Roumania.

The speech of Mr. Gladstone in 1858 and that of Napoleon in 1859 show the interest taken by each in the Principalities. But between the Frenchman and Englishman there was no co-operation. Probably Mr. Gladstone would not have delivered his speech of May 4, had he known that an agreement existed between Napoleon and England. The common interest of Gladstone and Napoleon in Roumania shows how two thinking minds, with a widely different environment, may, each independently of the other, grasp the same principle. The principle here involved was that of Nationality. In the persevering efforts of Mr. Gladstone in the interest of Irish autonomy, we see how far he went in his endeavor to apply to Ireland the Nationality Principle. The failure of his attempt has perhaps a parallel in the failure of the negotiation which Napoleon undertook, in 1863, in behalf of Poland. Whether or how far the Nationality Principle is yet to be applied to Poland and Ireland is a question.

The juncture at which Napoleon made his statement respecting the Principalities — February, 1859 — is full of significance. The Italian War was at hand. Incidents which provoked or at least foreshadowed it — the remark made by Napoleon on New Year's Day to the Austrian ambassador, and the marriage of Prince Napoleon to Victor Emanuel's daughter — had recently occurred. Napoleon was now to lay the foundation of a larger national unity than that of the Principalities of the Danube. Italy, the State whose destinies were shaped in 1859, was, in one sense, the fatherland of France and Roumania. The relation of these three States merits a more careful analysis than it has received.

The double election of Prince Alexander was, as has been said, contrary to the intent of the Convention of 1858. Whether this election should be ratified, the powers must decide. Before the question came before them, Prince Alexander adopted measures which showed, as his election had shown, what the sentiment of the provinces was. To make this sentiment conspicuous was his design. Part of the troops of Moldavia were sent to garrison posts in Wallachia, while part of the Wallachian troops were stationed in Moldavia. The Wallachian cabinet of Prince Alexander contained a Moldavian, and his Moldavian cabinet contained a Wallachian.

The tenacity with which the Principalities adhered to their purpose, and the support which they received from France and other States, did not fail of effect. In April, 1859, another conference met in Paris. All the powers, except Austria, urged upon Turkey the recognition of Prince Alexander as sovereign of both States. This recognition, however, they proposed as an exceptional step: it was not

to apply to the successors of Prince Alexander. The War
of 1859 broke out while the conference continued, and its
sittings were suspended. Three of the parties to the conference were parties to the war. Let us recur for a moment
to the scope of the Italian War. Its sudden termination at
Villafranca disappointed many. Yet its results are among
the most liberal of the nineteenth century. It exerted a
vast influence in favor of the Nationality Principle, chiefly
in Italy, but not in Italy alone. To this influence was due
in part the annexation of the Ionian Islands to Greece,
and the expulsion of the Turks from all the fortified posts,
including the fortress of Belgrade, which they still held in
Servia. Nor was the war without effect in the Principalities themselves. The beginning of hostilities interrupted,
as we have seen, the Paris conference. Prior to the cam-
paign of 1859 Austria was the only power which supported
Turkey in her refusal to recognize Alexander as sovereign
of both Moldavia and Wallachia. Owing to her defeat,
Austria yielded. The conference resumed its sittings, and
on the 6th of September all the powers acted in unison.
The recognition of Alexander as prince of both Principalities, subject to the stipulation that this grant should not
apply to his successors, was accorded by the sultan. But
the influence of the Italian War was not limited to the
Italian and Balkan peninsulas. It was felt in Germany;
and to that influence, in part, must be ascribed the down-
fall of Napoleon.

If we start with 1855 in the case of Roumania, and 1859
in that of Italy, and trace the emperor's course, we find two
lines of policy (subject to obstacles and interruptions, sometimes of like, sometimes of unlike nature) which were in
essence the same. The basis was the Principle of Nationality. As regards the obstacles met with in the emperor's
Eastern and Western policy, let us note a distinction.

His policy in the East was consistently and quietly
pursued. In France no opposition was found. Not so in

the case of his Italian policy. To this great opposition existed in France. Thiers became its chief spokesman. This opposition could scarcely fail to influence the emperor. The battle of Mentana shows how far at times his policy ran counter to the Italians.*

Let us revert to the Danube. The relation of the Principalities to each other resembled at this time that which exists between the Kingdom of Hungary and the rest of the Austrian Empire. Two legislatures existed, but a bond of union was found in the person of the sovereign.

The growth of the Nationality Principle in Austria and in Roumania has been effected through processes precisely opposite. Austria consists of several nationalities; and the tendency has been to give them greater independence. In Roumania there is only one nationality : here the tendency has been to unite the parts. A centrifugal force acted in the one case, a centralizing force in the other ; but the result is the same.

In October, 1860, upon the advice of the French government, Prince Alexander visited Constantinople, where he made a favorable impression. He stated to the Porte and to the representatives of the powers the inconveniences which an executive union of the Principalities involved, if clogged by two ministries and two legislative assemblies ; and, after his return to Bucharest, he formally communicated to the Turkish government his views. These, we need not say, were also Napoleon's. They were recommended by the French government to the Turkish ; and in 1861 the Porte sent to the powers a firman, in which it granted for the lifetime of Prince Alexander a union of the legislatures of the Principalities. On Dec. 23, 1861,

* Respecting the hostility in France to Napoleon's policy Charles de Mazade may be consulted. In his biography of Cavour, " Le Comte de Cavour," p. 242, he says, " La politique qui s'était déclarée depuis le 1er janvier soulevait, dans une partie de la société française, dans le monde religieux, dans l'ancien monde parlementaire et même dans une certaine classe des amis de l'empire, un tourbillon d'opposition." We might perhaps ask whether this opposition did not influence Napoleon, as the reluctance, if not hostility, of the North to emancipation influenced Mr. Lincoln.

the union of Moldavia and Wallachia was proclaimed at Bucharest. Thus was effected the legislative union of the Principalities, as two years before a union had been effected in the person of the sovereign.

The descendants of the colonists of Trajan chose a name for themselves which recalled the greatness of their origin. In his proclamation Prince Alexander named the new State *Roumania.**

In the same year, 1861, *in which the Principality of Roumania was established, the Kingdom of Italy was established also.* Not a few may aver — and who can dispute it? — that Napoleon's policy in behalf of these States, Italy and Roumania, was due in part to the fact that both are Latin. Each, in common with France, Spain, and Portugal, speaks a tongue derived from that of Rome.

The circumstance may be noted that, as long as Count Cavour lived, he supported Napoleon's policy in favor of the Latin Principalities of Turkey.† Nor should we fail to add that Cavour sent 15,000 Sardinian troops to the Crimea, so that Italy, both by diplomacy and arms, contributed to the enfranchisement of Roumania.

Let us rapidly sketch the events which ensued.

In 1863 the convents of Roumania were confiscated. In carrying out this policy, the Roumanian government was supported by France and Italy.‡ The French government finally induced the powers to sanction this act on condition that the confiscated convents should be indemnified, and a sum of 35,000,000 francs was voted for this purpose.

In 1864 occurred a reform of wider scope. Prince Alexander had vainly endeavored to induce the legislature to

---

* The Roumanians trace their origin as a people to the conquest of Dacia by Trajan, A.D. 103. Broken piers of the bridge which Trajan built and upon which he crossed the Danube are still seen beneath the water. The language of Roumania shows its derivation from the Latin, while wholly dissimilar tongues are spoken in the surrounding States. In Roumania the language and the vigor of Rome survive.

† "Le Comte de Cavour," by Charles de Mazade, p. 178.

‡ *Annuaire des Deux Mondes* for 1862-63, p. 681.

abolish the feudal obligations to which the peasantry were still subject. By means of a *coup d'état* which — save that no bloodshed occurred — recalls that of Napoleon, he dissolved the legislature and appealed to the people. The *coup d'état* was ratified by a great majority, and the emancipation of the peasants followed. More than 400,000 became proprietors of the soil. An English writer, James Samuelson, published in 1882 a work entitled " Roumania, Past and Present." In his preface he states that one of his purposes was to lay before his countrymen an account of the reform of 1864. The successful manner in which the land question had been settled, and facts therewith connected, might, he thought, be profitably considered in connection with the land question in Ireland.

But we have not asked in what manner the Revolution in the Roumanian government, which the *coup d'état* effected,— a revolution which increased the authority of the prince, — was recognized by Turkey. Prince Alexander, recalling the success of his former journey to Constantinople, again went thither; and, through his efforts and those of the French ambassador, the Marquis of Moustier, the change in the government of Roumania was ratified by the Porte and the powers.

The relation of Roumania to France and other States subsequent to the Crimean War is well described in an extract from the Constantinople correspondence of the New York *Tribune:* * " France and Italy have sought to make these provinces independent of Turkey. England has, of course, done her best to strengthen the power of Turkey, and repress any tendencies toward independent action. Russia is determined to annex these provinces to her own territory. Turkey wishes to retain them with as little trouble and expense as possible. The provinces themselves desire to become an independent kingdom. Consequently, French policy has been triumphant; and, to the dismay of England,

* New York *Tribune*, July 14, 1864.

Prince Couza has been doing very much as he liked, without regard to treaties or anything else."

The following reference occurs to the reforms just mentioned. The statement, however, as to the real estate of the Principality is much exaggerated. " Prince Couza first confiscated all the property of the Greek monasteries, which owned about half the real estate in the Principality; and, then, having turned the assembly into the street at the point of the bayonet, he annulled the constitution, and freed all the serfs in the provinces." *

The writer predicts that Prince Couza, "strong in his faith in Napoleon," would go on and do as he chose. To do as we choose often succeeds admirably, but sometimes the proceeding comes to a sudden termination.

One of the purposes of Alexander, briefly stated, was to assimilate the civilization of the Principality to that of Western Europe. Among the reforms of this period, besides those already noted, were the establishment of schools, the partial introduction of the Gregorian calendar, and the adoption of the metric system of weights and measures. But the statesmanship of the prince was not without defect. The finances of the State had been mismanaged.

In February, 1866, Prince Alexander was deposed. No one of his countrymen had done so much as he toward achieving the union of the Principalities and introducing reforms. But, though an admirable reformer, he was a voluptuary. His deposition was owing partly to this latter fact, partly to the fact that the people of Roumania were determined to have a foreigner for sovereign. So fixed was the purpose of Roumania to connect herself with the rest of

---

* The liberation of the peasants was effected by means of a decree issued by Prince Alexander prior to the meeting of the legislature, which was elected after the *coup d'état*. This decree had the force of law. After the *coup d'état* of 1851 a like state of affairs existed in France. Between the *coup d'état* and the opening of the Chambers in March, 1852, the decrees of Napoleon had the force of law. The decree which liberated the peasants in Roumania we might regard as part of the *coup d'état* itself. From one point of view we may compare the emancipation proclamation of President Lincoln to the decree of Prince Alexander. Each was an act of the executive, not of the legislature. West India emancipation was due to Parliament.

Europe by a dynastic tie that, when Alexander was elected Hospodar of Moldavia in 1859, he signed an agreement to relinquish the sovereignty in favor of a foreign prince, should the union of the Principalities be accomplished. The prince seems to have had a presentiment of his fall. A few weeks before it occurred, the Chambers were opened; and in his message he observed that he had received the sovereign power as a sacred trust, and was ready to relinquish it in favor of a foreign prince. The election of a foreign prince, it will be recalled, constituted the second of the propositions submitted by Napoleon to the powers in 1855. After the deposition of Alexander the legislature proceeded to choose his successor.

The first choice fell upon the Count of Flanders, brother of the King of Belgium. The count having declined, the next candidate was Prince Charles of Hohenzollern. The relations of France and Prussia at this time — prior to the war of 1866 — were not unfriendly; but it was thought that Napoleon might object to a Hohenzollern prince. Bratiano, one of the chiefs of the liberal party in Roumania, was in Paris, and laid the matter before the emperor. Not only he made no objection: he suggested to the Roumanian government to offer Prince Charles the crown; and this was done. Accurately stated, Napoleon's suggestion (*Anregung*) was that the Roumanian government should propose Prince Charles to the people as their prince.* That the prince, when elected, was chosen by a *plébiscite*, was owing perhaps to the form of this proposal.

At the Prussian court there were influences both favorable to the prince's acceptance and unfavorable. His father, Prince Anthony, whose part in the negotiations which preceded the war of 1870 is well known, was favorably disposed. The crown prince observed to Prince Charles that the fact that France had brought forward the candidature was the only disturbing circumstance. France,

* Memoirs of the King of Roumania, vol. i. p. 3.

having conferred a favor, might expect it to be returned.
Prince Charles replied that he did not think Napoleon had in
view such a policy. In his opinion the French sovereign was
influenced rather by the relationship which existed between
his Majesty and the Hechingen branch of the Hohenzollerns
than by any selfish considerations.* Prince Frederick
Charles advised the prince to decline the offer, not thinking
the position which he would hold in Roumania — that of
a prince tributary to the sultan — a position worthy of him.
The King of Prussia occupied an attitude of reserve. When
Prince Charles referred to the Roumanian question, his
Majesty *erwähnte mit keinem Worte*.

At Bucharest it was decided to proceed with the election,
and also that it should take place as a *plébiscite*. The
Chambers which had elected the Count of Flanders had
been dissolved. The voting occupied seven days, from
April 14 to April 20, and resulted in 685,969 votes in the
affirmative and 224 in the negative. April 20 was the
birthday of Prince Charles, and also that of Napoleon III.
Even after the triumphant election of the prince the King
of Prussia seemed almost neutral. He determined to exert
no direct influence upon the decision, yes or no, which the
prince was now to take.†

The election was virtually unanimous, and Prince Charles
determined to accept. He set out for Roumania, and wrote
to Napoleon III. as follows : —

"I have set out, trusting in God and your Majesty."

He also wrote, "I dare to hope that your Majesty will
kindly continue to Roumania and her prince his powerful
protection, which brings to life and sustains oppressed
nationalities."

* The kinship referred to was due to the marriage of the Princess Josephine, a grand-
daughter of the Empress Josephine and daughter of Napoleon's uncle, Prince Eugene,
to the Prince of Hohenzollern-Hechingen. Subsequently, in a letter to Napoleon,
Prince Charles refers to this relationship. Alluding to his Majesty he says, " J'ai en
moi de son sang."

† Memoirs of King Charles of Roumania, vol. i. p. 27.

In this letter the prince ascribes his election to the fact that the people of Roumania remembered his relationship, to Napoleon.*

A romantic circumstance attaches to the journey of the prince. He was an officer in the Prussian army; and, owing to the hostility of Austria to his candidature, he traversed that empire under an assumed name. The prince was a lieutenant in the dragoons of the Guard, and exchanged his uniform for a civilian's dress. He went up the Rhine to Basle and Zürich in Switzerland, and thence through Munich to Vienna. Here he took a train down the Danube, and waited at Bazias, near the Roumanian frontier, for the steamer. May 18 he went on board, taking, as a precaution, a second-class passage. Bratiano arrived from Paris at the same time, was informed of the presence of his prince, and notified that he would have to ignore him entirely for a while. When they landed in Roumania at Turnu Severin, the very spot where Trajan built his bridge, their restraint was thrown off. On the 22d of May the prince entered Bucharest, where he was greeted with loud acclamations, and flowers were strewn in his path.

This journey of the prince is connected in a strange manner with Napoleon's destinies. Reference has previously been made to the candidature of Prince Leopold, the brother of Prince Charles, to the throne of Spain in 1870. After the withdrawal of this candidature, Napoleon wrote a letter to his minister for foreign affairs, in which he insisted that the withdrawal, under the attending circumstances, was not sufficient. The King of Prussia ought to agree, he said, that the candidature should not be repeated. He ought to agree not to allow Prince Leopold "to follow the example of his brother, and set off some fine day for

---

* This letter and others are found in a German work, the "Memoirs of King Charles of Roumania," published at Stuttgard in 1894. The contents are described as *Aufzeichnungen eines Augenzeugen*. These two volumes are full of evidence of the relation between Napoleon III. on the one hand and Roumania and Prince Charles on the other.

Spain." Thus the romance of the journey down the Danube which enhanced, we may suppose, the enthusiasm of the prince's reception in Bucharest, was one of many circumstances which helped bring on the war of 1870 and destroy Napoleon.*

Let us return to 1866. There has probably been more policy than sincerity in those professions of interest often put forth by Russia as to the Balkan States. To prove this, it is not necessary to refer to the present relations of Russia and Bulgaria. The events of 1866 tell the same story. Although the policy of Russia toward Roumania had thus far in most cases coincided with that of France, yet on this occasion Russia declared herself opposed both to the election of a foreign prince and to the continued union of the Moldo-Wallachian State! It scarcely served the designs of Russia to have an independent, vigorous nationality planted upon the road from Moscow to the Golden Horn.†

To explain more fully the attitude of Russia and also of Turkey in 1866, we may call to mind that, when the union of the Principalities was effected, its recognition by the Turkish government applied to the reign of Prince Alexander only. Upon his deposition the question once more became open. The friends of union believed that — although, in a strict sense, the union was only temporary — it was destined to become lasting. The powers hostile to union — Russia, Austria, and Turkey — hoped that an opportunity

---

* A misapprehension as to the war of 1870 may here be noted. Many suppose that the first demand made by the French emperor just before the war was granted. It was not. The requisition was that the King of Prussia, who had sanctioned the candidature of Prince Leopold, should advise or order him to abandon it. But, when it had been abandoned, the Prussian government stated that the action of the prince was voluntary, and that the King of Prussia had nothing to do with it. See "La France et la Prusse avant la Guerre," by the Duc de Gramont, p. 118. We need not discuss Napoleon's course. It is, nevertheless, true that the second demand was made in order to *provide a substitute* for the part of the first which had not been granted, and which, in the nature of the case, could not be granted when the candidature had been withdrawn.

† The population of the Kingdom of Roumania, at present 5,800,000, exceeds that of Sweden.

had arrived which would enable them to split the State into its original halves.

The choice of a Hohenzollern prince was fortunate. Such was the hostility of the 'Porte that troops were despatched to the Danube, and a military occupation of the Principality was threatened. A few weeks after the arrival of Prince Charles in Roumania, however, the battle of Sadowa occurred. The prestige acquired by Prussia overthrew the hopes of Russia and Turkey, and hastened the recognition by all the powers of the newly elected sovereign. Since the fall of France in 1870 the Roumanians, while cherishing a remembrance of the services rendered by her, can afford to felicitate themselves that their sovereign is a German.

By the choice of Prince Charles the second of Napoleon's propositions submitted to the powers in 1855 was carried out. The union of the Principalities had been accomplished in 1861. A foreign prince was chosen hereditary sovereign in 1866.

We are not to suppose that, upon the acquisition of the crown by Prince Charles, Roumania became independent. The Principality continued to recognize the suzerainty of the sultan, to pay a fixed tribute, and to owe military service. It was not until after the Turco-Russian War of 1878, in which the prince and army of Roumania took an honorable part, that the tie between Turkey and Roumania was sundered. At this time the Principality was erected into a kingdom. The death of Napoleon occurred in 1873, about half-way between the election of Prince Charles as Prince of Roumania in 1866 and his assumption of the regal title in 1881.

If the services of Napoleon to Roumania were many and effective, at times his judgment may have been lacking. At least, it seems to have wavered. After the revolution which deposed Prince Alexander, the Italian government, fixed upon the acquisition of Venetia, urged upon the em-

peror the following scheme,— that Austria should give up
Venetia, and accept instead the Principalities of the Danube. The German historian Von Sybel tells us that Napoleon "had scarcely favored such an idea." *

However, at present he seemed ready to indorse it, in
part at least, and communicated it to the powers. This
scheme, as far as Roumania was concerned, amounted to a
transfer from the Ottoman to the Austrian Empire. If such
a transfer seemed contrary to the interests of Roumania, an
argument nevertheless may be alleged in its favor. If we
consider that the population of Roumania was about 4,500,-
000, and that the parts of Austria adjacent to Roumania
contained a Roumanian population of 2,600,000 (a fair majority of the population of Transylvania is Roumanian), it
might be urged that an eventual union of all parts of the
Roumanian nationality might be promoted by the annexation. Austria, however, objected; and so did the other
powers. Austria, perhaps, objected for a reason similar to
that which led Napoleon, it would seem, to favor the project,
— an apprehension that, if the 7,000,000 Roumanians of
Austria and Roumania were brought under one government,
an agitation would be started to bring into closer union all
parts of the Roumanian race, and establish some such kingdom of Roumania as that which we have at present, of
which the correspondence of the *Tribune* spoke. Of what
use was it to extract from the foot of Austria a thorn in the
shape of an unruly Latin province, if a fresh one were im-
planted in its place? It is possible that Napoleon's indorse-
ment of the scheme was owing to a wish to conciliate
Austria. If not successful in one respect, he may have
been in another. How was the cession of Venetia to Italy
effected? By means of the treaty of June 12, 1866, Venetia
was ceded by Austria to Napoleon, and by Napoleon trans-
ferred to its rightful owners. If he failed to liberate Venice
in 1859, he had, to say the least, a hand in the liberation of
1866.

* Founding of the German Empire, vol. iv. p. 334.

The scheme above referred to has been stated, in order that all needful facts may be before us with respect to Napoleon and Roumania,— those wholly to his credit and others of which so much perhaps might not be said.*

Let us note a further circumstance with regard to the negotiations of 1866. After the deposition of Prince Alexander a conference, as on previous occasions, met in Paris. But it did not amount to much. Early in May it reminded the people of Roumania that, according to the Convention of 1858, the prince to be elected was to be a native prince. At this very time Napoleon had assented to the candidature of Prince Charles of Hohenzollern, and this prince had been elected. If Roumania and Napoleon worked one way and the conference another, there was a fair chance for disagreement. The battle of Sadowa was worth a dozen conferences.

If Prince Charles was chosen April 20 by means of a *plébiscite*, this election was followed by another less revolutionary in form. He was chosen by a constituent assembly May 13. It has been observed that at the time of the *coup d'état* and the liberation of the peasants the constitution of the State became more autocratic. The *Annuaire des Deux Mondes* remarks that this autocratic constitution resembled that of the Second Empire. According to the same authority the constitution substituted in 1866 for this autocracy resembled the constitution of Belgium. We may call to mind that the first offer of the crown was made to a Belgian prince.

Having reviewed the events which took place between

---

* Mr. Fyffe alleges (History of Modern Europe, vol. iii. p. 235) that during the Congress of Paris in 1856 Napoleon "had revived his project of incorporating the Danubian Principalities with Austria in return for the cession of Lombardy." Let us suppose that Napoleon suggested this scheme as a solution which deserved consideration. Mr. Fyffe is, however, in error when, having observed that Austria declined the proposition, he states that "Napoleon consequently entered upon a new Eastern policy"; namely, by proposing the union of the Principalities ' into a single State." *The original proposition* to unite the provinces was made *by Napoleon* at Vienna, March 26, 1855. This policy could not have been "new" in 1856.

the French propositions of 1855 and the carrying out of the second in 1866, let us note certain circumstances which refer to later occurrences or to Roumania at present.

That Napoleon continued to interest himself in the Principality appears from the following despatches which passed between himself and Prince Charles.

The Jews of Roumania, like those of Russia, have suffered at times from persecution. In 1867, the year after the accession of the prince, France, England, and Austria remonstrated against certain measures which had severely oppressed Jews accused of vagrancy. The Roumanian government replied that the matter should be minutely investigated. Napoleon, at the time of this intervention, sent from Paris the following despatch to Prince Charles: "I ought not to allow Your Highness to be ignorant of the manner in which public opinion here is stirred up respecting the persecutions to which, it is said, the Jews of Moldavia are exposed. I cannot believe that the enlightened government of Your Highness authorizes measures so contrary to humanity and civilization."

The prince answered: "Your Majesty may be assured that I have no less solicitude than yourself for the Jewish population. The measures which the government thought it ought to take have nothing exceptional about them and belong to the common law. I shall have a severe investigation, however, to ascertain whether subaltern officials have not exceeded their instructions. The guilty shall be punished with all the rigor of the laws."

This intervention seems at least to have lessened the grievances of the Jews. But a strict enforcement of the "common law" was not sufficient. For over fifty years the laws had discriminated against the Jews. Finally, it was stipulated in the Treaty of Berlin in 1878 that the recognition by the powers of the independence of Roumania was conditioned upon the recognition by that State of *the equality of all sects before the law* (Arts. 43–45).

On setting out to consider the part of Napoleon in the liberation of Roumania, the first circumstance noted referred to the funeral rites which occurred at his death. In the "Memoirs of King Charles" we read as follows (vol. ii. p. 300): "15 January. In the Metropolitan Church as well as in all the churches of the country took place the funeral service [*Trauergottesdienst*] which had been ordered in honor of the Emperor Napoleon."

These rites were observed on the same day, Jan. 15, 1873, on which occurred Napoleon's funeral at Chiselhurst.

Under the date January 10, on which day the news arrived of the emperor's decease, we find the following: "The Prince and Princess send to the widowed Empress and Imperial Prince the expression of their affectionate sympathy. In his own name the Prince adds: 'Pour mo le souvenir des bontés de l'Empereur est à jamais gravé dans mon cœur.'"

Under this date we also read, "Prince Charles is deeply affected; and throughout the whole country is manifested a spontaneous, sincere grief at the death of the former protector of the Principle of Nationality [*Nationalitätsprinzips*], to whom Roumania owes her existence as a State."

A few years after Napoleon's death the army of the new State was summoned to the field.

At the siege of Plevna the Roumanian army greatly distinguished itself. Prince Charles was commander-in-chief of the united Russian and Roumanian forces. In 1881 President Grévy of France sent the prince, who at this time assumed the title of king, the decoration known as the military medal. In his reply Prince Charles says: "I feel myself the more flattered by this distinction on your part because it is reflected upon my whole army, which knew how to perform its duty on the field of honor, commanded by brave officers who owe their military training [*leurs connaissances militaires*] in large part to the schools of France."

It thus appears that one of the services which Napoleon

rendered was the permission to have officers of the Roumanian army educated in the French military schools.

Another circumstance relates to the flag of Roumania. It is a tricolor, and is in fact the same as the French, save that a yellow stripe in the Roumanian replaces the white.

One result of the intimate relation between the States has been the use of the French language by the educated classes in Roumania. An authority already cited, Mr. Samuelson, says, "French is almost the universal language of the middle classes." Among the publications of the late George M. Towle is a political and historical sketch of Roumania. Respecting Bucharest he says, "No one is worthy of social consideration who is not familiar with French." Edward King, well known as a journalist and author, wrote, "In Roumania there is a little France, although it is ruled by a German king." * A further indication of the influence of France is found in the fact that the code of Roumania is based upon the *Code Napoléon.*

In summing up the services which Napoleon III. rendered to Roumania, let us, first of all, bear in mind that in a special sense he represented France. One is reminded of the saying of Louis XIV.,—"L'état, c'est moi." When we find that the French government pursued a specific course, this means that Napoleon pursued it. In an extract already quoted Mr. Gladstone referred to the emperor as "the absolute sovereign of France." And yet this absolute sovereignty reposed upon universal suffrage. In the case of Napoleon's Roumanian policy no hostility, as we have seen, existed in France. We are even more certain of seeing an act of the emperor in each act of his government than in the case of Italy, for here Napoleon encountered opposition: his course was deflected from that which he would otherwise have pursued.†

* Boston *Journal,* Aug. 29, 1885.

† In the above the writer does not mean to eulogize autocratic government. One of the best things that Napoleon did was to give up, to the extent to which he did, between 1860 and 1870 (beginning with the famous decree of Nov. 24, 1860), autocracy. If, however, in any case his autocratic power was justly used, let us note the fact.

Briefly stated, Napoleon's services to Roumania were these. In laying before the powers during the siege of Sebastopol the propositions of 1855 — those in favor of the union of the Principalities and the sovereignty of a foreigner . — he advocated measures called for by the interests and the people of the Moldo-Wallachian States.*

The propositions submitted at Vienna; the first of these, submitted twelve months later at Paris; a renewed declaration of the French government in favor of union, Feb. 5, 1857; Napoleon's visit to Osborne; the cancelling of the Moldavian elections and the Convention of 1858,— these were the first steps. The final achievement of union was effected, partly through the election of Colonel Alexander Couza just before the war of 1859, partly by the consolidation of both legislatures and the assumption of the name Roumania two years later.

Finally, the proposition respecting the sovereignty of a foreign prince, advocated by France both in 1855 and 1858, was realized through the deposition of Prince Alexander and the election of Prince Charles in 1866.

Owing to the English alliance and the Crimean War, conditions were supplied without which Napoleon's plan could scarcely have succeeded. The lessening of the prestige of Russia and her exhaustion consequent upon the war were circumstances not inimical to the growth of the emancipated State, one which Russia had occupied at the beginning of the war and had hoped to make part of her dominions.

The Treaty of Paris, which closed the Crimean War, favored the interests and autonomy of the Moldo-Wallachian States. Owing to the stipulation which provided for elec-

---

* Evidence enough has perhaps been given that Napoleon correctly interpreted the interests and will of the people. The following might be added. In January, 1859, a few months after the conclusion of the Convention of 1858, the Moldavian assembly voted a declaration in which it stated that *the union of the Principalities under a foreign prince* "has been, is, and always will be the most active, ardent, and universal wish of the Roumanian nation."

tions in the Principalities and for an expression of the preferences of the people, Napoleon was able, to a large extent, to introduce those preferences into the Convention of 1858. Thus was the way prepared for the final union of Moldavia and Wallachia.

That provision of the Treaty of Paris which abolished the Russian protectorate of 1829, substituting for it a joint protectorate of the powers, had great value. While nominally a joint protectorate, it was virtually French. This instrumentality Napoleon constantly employed.

In reviewing the events recorded, we cannot fail to note in how hearty a manner the governments of France and Roumania worked together, whether with regard to a reform of the highest moment, the union of the provinces, or to lesser and yet important changes, such as the confiscation of the convents and the enfranchisement of the peasants.

A reference to the scheme brought forward by Italy in 1866 with regard to Austria, Venetia, and Roumania, is hardly called for. Napoleon could scarcely have considered the plan feasible save upon the condition of its acceptance by both Austria and Roumania. Austria never accepted it; and this killed the plan whenever it was suggested.

A divided State, legally subject to Turkey, but occupied at the beginning of the Crimean War by the Russian arms, has become a free, united, and prosperous kingdom. Not a few personalities, historical influences and historical tendencies have contributed to this result. That among personalities the first place belongs to Napoleon, we cannot doubt. Here the testimony of the liberated State should be considered,— the funeral rites of 1873.

One noteworthy circumstance connected with the services of Napoleon to Moldo-Wallachia is the fact that for several years after the inauguration of his policy Great Britain opposed him. His policy was liberal, hers the reverse. Mr. Gladstone was an exception among British statesmen, and, we may also add, Lord John Russell. Comparing the statesmen of England on the one hand and Napoleon on the other, Napoleon had the greater political and moral insight. There is a point of view not yet touched upon with regard to the emperor and the Crimean War. Some have averred (Mr. Kinglake's History, vol. i. p. 49) that Napoleon's purpose in the negotiations with Turkey, which occurred in 1851 and 1852,— negotiations which resulted in granting to France and the Latin Church certain privileges as to the shrines in Palestine,— was to provoke war. That the carrying up to Bethlehem of a silver star adorned with the arms of France (Kinglake's History, vol. i. pp. 51, 53) should have caused the siege of Sebastopol may seem improbable. But the granting of this and other privileges did provoke Russia; and six months later, in July, 1853, the invasion of Turkey began.

If it was Napoleon's design by inaugurating the Turkish negotiations prior to the *coup d'état* to bring about a Russian war, if it was his design to pursue in behalf of Moldo-Wallachia the policy which he did pursue, he possessed a degree of foresight and sagacity for which not many have given him credit. At all events, if Napoleon did not provoke the Crimean War, he knew how to use it in the interest of justice and freedom.

We have reviewed facts which relate to the Crimean War and Napoleon III. Mr. A. D. Vandam, in a series of articles in the *North American Review*, says (May, 1895) that the Crimean War "was undertaken, not for political, but for social purposes; namely, to give the new empress the sponsor she lacked face to face with the sovereigns of Europe." Let us imagine that the emperor cherished this design. He cherished others. The verdict of history must be that to the fall of Sebastopol and the masterly policy which Napoleon pursued between 1855 and 1866 the establishment of Roumania as a free State is chiefly due.

If George Washington or Abraham Lincoln had pursued for eleven years such a policy and effected such results, should we not eulogize the purpose and achievement?

Toward the close of the empire the services which it rendered to oppressed States seem to have attracted the attention of Anglo-Saxon writers. Our historian George Bancroft wrote,—our sketch begins with these noble lines,— Jan. 25, 1867 ; * " It is the glory of the French nation that it has on many decisive occasions put forth its strength on the side of liberty ; and the Netherlands, the United States, and Italy bear witness to her effective services as the defender of nationalities and the soldier of freedom."

To the services rendered by France in the instances named should be added those of Napoleon III. in the liberation of Roumania.

The policy of Napoleon, both in Roumania and Italy, was based upon the Nationality Principle. If we consider his policy in other cases,— in the difficulty between Prussia and Switzerland in 1857, which resulted in the abdication by the King of Prussia of all his rights as sovereign of Neuchâtel; the difficulty between Prussia and France as to Luxemburg in 1867, which resulted in the evacuation of Luxemburg by Prussia and the demolition of the fortress ; if we consider the case of Savoy and Nice; if we consider the fact that in the Sleswick-Holstein Question the emperor favored the Germans of those provinces in their wish to belong to Germany, and, in like manner, the Danes of northern Sleswick in their wish to continue Danes; if we consider an instance in which the emperor's policy failed, the joint intervention of the French, British, and Austrian governments in behalf of Poland at the time of the insurrection of 1863 ; if, finally, we consider the question which arose between Servia and Turkey as to Belgrade and other fortresses in 1862 and 1866,— we find in every instance that the emperor's policy rested upon the Principle of Nationality.†

* Letter read at a meeting in New York in sympathy with the revolted Cretans.

† In two speeches made in the Chamber, March 14 and 18, 1867, Thiers arraigned Napoleon's government because of its services to Nationality. The imperial government, he alleged, had substituted for the principle of the balance of power the Principle

Mr. John Fiske, in an article in the *Atlantic Monthly*, April, 1877, entitled "The Races of the Danube," gives an excellent definition of what constitutes a nationality, and also designates the relation between the Principle of Nationality and the Eastern Question. He says,—the Italics are our own : "In the famous Eastern Question, which now for half a century has alternately threatened and disturbed the peace of Europe, may be noted two aspects of a process which under great variety of conditions has been going on over European territory ever since the dawn of authentic history. *The formation of a nationality* — that is, of a community of men sufficiently connected in interests and dis ciplined in social habits to live together peacefully under laws of their own making — *has been the leading aspect of this process*, in which the work of civilization has hitherto largely consisted.* But along with this, as a correlative aspect, has gone the pressure exerted against the community by an external mass of undisciplined barbarism ever on the alert to break over the fluctuating barrier that has warded it off."

Ever since authentic history began, Mr. Fiske tells us, this process has gone on. The Principle of Nationality has asserted itself, and "barbarism" has fought against it. During this whole period no instance perhaps has occurred

---

of Nationality. To this principle he referred as "ce principe, déplorable à mon avis, des nationalités." It is true that Thiers's objection to the principle lay in his forecast that the devotion of Napoleon to it would raise up enemies to France. Nor were his sombre predictions long in coming to pass. The question has not occurred to Americans as forcibly as it might whether France since 1870 has not deserved our sympathy precisely because her overthrow was due in part to her services to Nationality.

As regards the two speeches of Thiers, Gustave Rothan, in his work "L' Affaire du Luxembourg," gives their gist in one sentence, (p. 193). The imperial government, Thiers said, "had substituted for the principle of the balance of power the Principle of Nationality, of which it had made itself on every occasion the devoted champion and persevering apostle."

* True to the above definition of nationality, which refers neither to origin nor language, Mr. Fiske, in an introduction to a work by Mr. Harold Murdock, published in 1889, "The Reconstruction of Europe from the Rise to the Fall of the Second Empire," observes that "the annexation of Alsace-Lorraine by Germany was really a violation of what is the sound basis of the sacredness of nationalities."

of the genesis of a nationality fraught with greater interest than the genesis of Roumania.*

The irruption of the Nationality Principle into the Balkan peninsula was a great event. One even greater was its irruption shortly after into the Italian. To the east and west of the Adriatic, Napoleon grasped the issues, and planted them upon this principle. As the inspiration of his thinking and doing, Napoleon chose a principle of liberty,—according to Mazzini the first principle of the century. Not a bad way of judging the value of Napoleon's work in Roumania is to estimate it in the light of Mr. Fiske's words respecting the Eastern Question and Nationality Principle.

The significance of the Nationality Principle applied to Roumania largely consists in the fact that this principle was applied to the Eastern Question. September 8 the Malakoff fell. September 8 is one of the red-letter days of freedom. The fall of this fortress meant that the Principle of Conquest, Russia's principle, was worsted. The arms and diplomacy of the Second Empire made noble preparation for the further growth of the Nationality Principle, which occurred after the war of 1878, not only in Roumania, but in Servia and Bulgaria. We should note especially the steadfastness and advance of Bulgaria in spite of Russia.

In an article contributed to the *Edinburgh Review* by Mr. Gladstone immediately after Sedan, he refers to the ten years which followed the Crimean War as a period of "towering influence, prosperity, and power." † During this period Napoleon carried out in the Balkan peninsula the process of liberation which we have considered. Respecting Napoleon, Mr. Gladstone says, "Two services he has conferred upon the world." One referred to the liberation

* Mr. Fiske uses the words "undisciplined barbarism." "Undisciplined" could not be applied to Russia in 1855. Had it not been for the discipline of her civilization and arms, the defence of Sebastopol would not have been what it was.

† "Germany, France, and England," *Edinburgh Review*, October, 1870.

of Italy, the other to the treaty known at the time as the Cobden Treaty, but which, in the language of American politics, we might describe as the tariff-reform or reciprocity treaty of 1860. Whatever the merits of this treaty, we might have more reason perhaps to name, *if we emphasize two services*, the liberation of Italy and the liberation of Roumania. It does not often happen in the whole range of history that a prince or president emancipates two States. One is the more ready to ask why Mr. Gladstone did not associate the liberation of Italy and that of Roumania as Napoleon's achievements *par excellence* because he agreed with the emperor's Roumanian policy. In support of it he made a powerful speech.

It is useless to attempt to settle what matter of man Napoleon was till we know his acts. In any review of his reign nothing will appear so absurd as the way in which his Roumanian policy has been ignored. A remarkable series of events transpired between March, 1855, and May, 1866. Scarcely was the world aware of the fact that the world was being revolutionized, as far as the Eastern Question went and the adoption of the Nationality Principle as the chief factor in its settlement.

Let us cite an illustration of the manner in which these events have been suppressed. How happens it that Mr. Kinglake, in his history of the " Invasion of the Crimea," in eight volumes, omits all reference to the fact that Napoleon submitted to the powers the propositions, or plan, of 1855? This plan not one of the powers indorsed. France and Napoleon carried it out. *Mr. Kinglake devotes thirty-five pages to the proceedings of the Conference of Vienna before which the emperor's plan was laid, and even names the date, March 26, upon which it was submitted. To it he makes no reference.* What was Mr. Kinglake's motive? The question is complex. It relates to the attitude of England toward Roumania, to that of Napoleon, and to the views propounded by Mr. Kinglake as to the *coup d'état* and

Napoleon's character. Is it possible that our author was ignorant of the facts? The essence, one might almost say, and outcome of the Crimean War are found in the plan of 1855. Nevertheless, with reference to it and the grand policy which issued from it our historian is dumb.*

Lieutenant F. V. Greene, in his report to our government on "The Russian Army and its Campaigns in Turkey in 1877–1878," refers to the siege of Sebastopol as "the most famous perhaps of authentic sieges." The fame of this siege will become yet greater in proportion as the use to which it was put by France and Bonaparte is understood.†

A question as interesting as any which the independence of Roumania suggests is whether the popular estimate of Napoleon III. should not be revised. If Mazzini was a true prophet, if the Principle of Nationality has given its name to this century, it cannot be denied that Napoleon III., rather than any other man, was the champion of this principle.‡ It is the fashion with many to disparage, in comparison with the uncle, the nephew. The nephew has, nevertheless, one great advantage. The achievements of Napoleon I. were such a mixture, his services to despotism and freedom so combined, that, when he fell, the changes which he had made on the map of Europe perished with him. Exceptions we need not discuss. If expiation was made at Leipzig for the subjugation of the Tyrol, Napoleon's best work, on the other hand also perished — the Kingdom of Italy and that part of the Kingdom of Poland which he emancipated after Friedland.

It is the glory of Napoleon III., if he achieved any, that, taking as the key of his European policy a principle of liberty, that of nationality, he wrought with such success that

---

* See "Invasion of the Crimea," vol. vii. pp. 313 to 347, inclusive.

† Of course, Lieutenant Greene, in using the word "authentic," excludes sieges which, like that of Troy, are not authentic. Our author might have referred to the siege of Sebastopol as the most famous perhaps of all sieges, save the siege of Troy.

‡ With regard to Mazzini the following work should be consulted: "Joseph Mazzini: His Life and Writings, with an Introduction by William Lloyd Garrison," p. 87. Hurd & Houghton, 1872.

his noblest work, Italy and Roumania, survived him. No eclipse fell upon either, such as that which ruined the Grand Duchy of Warsaw and the Kingdom of Italy of Napoleon I. In lesser instances the work of Napoleon III. lasted. This we may say of the expulsion of Prussia from Switzerland in 1857, and from Luxemburg ten years later. Nor is reference needed to Savoy and Nice. The lasting character of his work, a work in behalf of nationality and freedom, is the glory of the man of Solferino and Sedan. It is not equally the glory of the man of Austerlitz and Waterloo.

If a revision of the popular estimate of Louis Napoleon is demanded, the facts to determine it do not relate to nationality only. Hugh McCulloch, twice our Secretary of the Treasury, published in the New York *Tribune* in 1875 a series of letters on finance. There were eleven, and they were written in London. They had special reference to our own finances, but the first two were entitled "The Finances of France." In the fourth, published in the *Tribune* May 8, 1875, the ex-Secretary refers to the period of the empire as one of "unexampled prosperity." Let us call to mind that the growth of private enterprise, which was the basis of this prosperity, achieved its greatest result in the Suez Canal, a work dedicated by its charter — and, in 1888, by European treaty — to neutrality and peace.* We may perhaps concede that in several respects Napoleon III. did not deserve ill of posterity: he deserved well.

Perhaps we might pardon, at least part way, the *coup d'état* if we measure its achievements.

It may be worth while to glance at the view of the *coup d'état* and the Revolution of 1848 presented by Renan. Both acts were acts of violence, in contempt of law. Renan despised them. But he makes a distinction. The Republican party of 1848, he says, was a turbulent, imperceptible minority. This minority set aside the will of the majority.

* The Suez Canal was the last achievement of the empire. It was inaugurated by the empress, Nov. 16, 1869, less than a year before Sedan.

The French, partly by the election of Napoleon, Dec. 10, 1848, and partly by the sanction which they gave to the *coup d'état*, overthrew the minority. They established the will of the people again. According to this view the usurpers were the men of 1848,— Victor Hugo and the rest. According to Renan the *coup d'état* possessed one element of freedom not found in the Revolution of 1848,— the right of the majority to govern.* The French had as much right perhaps to sanction the *coup d'état* as, twenty years later, they had to sanction Sedan.

The distinguished French Republican, Jules Simon, lately deceased, who after Sedan was a member of the Government of National Defence, seems to entertain like views. In a statement communicated to the *Gaulois* shortly before his death (reprinted in the weekly edition of the *Courrier des États-Unis*, April 25, 1896) he observes that the majority of those who voted for Louis Napoleon in December, 1848, expected a *coup d'état*. If so, they voted for him because they expected a *coup d'état* and wished it. Ought we to accuse Napoleon of perjury if he interpreted the vote which gave him so vast a majority — five millions against one and a half — in precisely the way in which those who elected him interpreted it; namely, as signifying that for the present he should be President of the republic, but that by and by he should upset the republic and establish the empire? Respecting his statement that most of those who elected Napoleon President expected a *coup d'état*, Simon observes, "Je l'ai déjà dit à la décharge du prince-président."

In the opinion of good judges no short History of France has greater merit than one in two volumes by a distinguished minister of Napoleon III., Victor Duruy. He occupied the post of minister of public instruction during most of the latter years of the empire. Ex-President Andrew D. White, of Cornell, whose acquaintance with French

* Renan's "Monarchie Constitutionnelle en France" may be consulted (pp. 62 to 67).

history is well known, says, "Of all the short summaries of French history, this is probably the best." In his "Manual of Historical Literature," ex-President C. K. Adams says that it is "beyond question the best History of France ever published in the short space of two volumes." Professor J. F. Jameson, of Brown University, writes that no better choice could be made than "the famous work of M. Duruy." Owing to the interest which Professor Jameson took in it, he added to an English translation a continuation which brings the work down from 1870 to 1889. He also prefixed an introductory notice, which consists of a short sketch of the author. To the administration of Duruy he refers as "this great administration." Again, referring to Duruy, he speaks of "his brilliant and extraordinarily fruitful official career." Most persons are not aware that so much was done under the Second Empire for popular education. Brief references to the educational work of Duruy are found in Professor Jameson's sketch. In this sketch the author says, " Duruy has himself told us that he never received from the emperor any other instructions than these words, in a letter written soon after his appointment: ' Maintain, as I do, an enthusiasm for all that is great and noble.' " The fact that Duruy acquiesced in what some might term so arrogant a claim,— acquiesced at least in part, — none will deny. Duruy was more intimate with the emperor than were most of his ministers. He assisted him in the preparation of his Life of Cæsar. Duruy was the better able thus to assist because of his familiarity with Roman history. His History of the Romans, which in its final shape occupies seven volumes, is probably the most complete and scholarly ever written.*

* To honor the man who in so able a manner had told the story of Rome, King Humbert of Italy presented to Duruy in 1885, on the completion of his history, a gold medal. It bore the following inscription: " Vittorio Duruy qui ausus est unus Gallorum omne Romanorum ævum explicare."

To preceding testimonies with respect to Duruy the writer adds the following, taken by permission from a letter written, July 22, 1885, by Andrew D. White, LL.D.: " There is one thing to be said which you do not mention. I have always thought that

If the claim of Napoleon as to his motives was acquiesced in by Duruy, as much may perhaps be said of Professor Jameson, the eulogist of Duruy. All human creatures have faults. In the case of Napoleon III. this was manifest enough. That, however, the chief aims of Napoleon's life were worthy aims, such as belong to true statesmanship, posterity, freed from certain prejudices of to-day, will perhaps admit. If what may be termed the old-fashioned view of Napoleon III., that of Kinglake and Victor Hugo, gives way to views more moderate, one evidence of the fact that Napoleon's aims were high is found in his astonishing services to a principle of freedom,—the Principle of Nationality. It is a singular fact that, if we look at the services of France to this principle and those of Napoleon III., no French writer has eulogized them more heartily than two foreigners,—our historian Mr. Bancroft and a prince of the House of Hohenzollern, the King of Roumania.

After the war of 1859 Mrs. Browning expressed a wish as to Napoleon :—

> " The praise of nations ready to perish
> Fall on him."

So much obscurity has rested upon the liberation of Roumania that we may doubt whether Mrs. Browning knew what she said. Did she know that her words applied both to Italy and to a second State, one on the Euxine? Who the liberator of Roumania was, Roumania never forgot.

At a banquet given in Boston, May 24, 1892, to Thomas Jefferson Coolidge, just appointed our minister to France, President Eliot of Harvard said, " I have always felt that we of the United States ought to have the opportunity to

---

the retention of Duruy as minister of public instruction was very creditable to the emperor. Duruy once told me that he was minister of public instruction for six years [1863–69], and that during the six years which had elapsed between his retiring from office and the date of our conversation there had been seven different ministers of public Instruction in France. That would seem to be somewhat creditable to the empire, as is the fact that a man of such fine character, powers, and ideal, was put into such a place."

pay France the enormous debt we owe her,— a debt incurred in war and unpaid; a greater debt incurred in peace,
also unpaid,— her philosophy and literature of the eigh-
teenth century. Jefferson was full of that French philosophy, and I doubt not our friend here inherits his due share
of that humane philosophy. And I hope he means to pay
this debt we owe to the country in which he is to represent
the United States."

One might ask whether it is not possible to pay, not this
debt, but part, if the facts stated in these pages are clearly
and honestly set forth. May we not contribute toward
paying our debt, if, as regards one of the great epochs of
French history, we substitute truth for its suppression and
facts for calumny? From an historian of the Second Empire, M. de La Gorce, the statement has been quoted that
the empire underwent the falsehood of adulation, and then
the falsehood of calumny. Is it not time that the falsehood
of calumny should cease? At least, ought not Americans
to desist, and leave to others a task which to others may
prove more congenial? An expression due in a special
sense to one of the clergymen of New England is, "Lend a
hand." The careers of few kings, presidents, or emperors
better exemplify it than that of Louis Napoleon. If we
consider what he did in behalf of freedom and nationality
in Italy and Roumania, not to mention Switzerland, Luxemburg, and Servia; if we neglect wholly the similar, if not
conspicuous, action of France as regards Poland and Hungary,— may we not acknowledge that few statesmen have
better deserved a title such as we may apply to Napoleon
III.? A great soldier he was not: a great *lend-a-hand*
emperor he was.

Let us compare Mrs. Browning's eulogium of Napoleon,

" The praise of nations ready to perish
Fall on him," *

* To Mrs. Browning's testimony as to Napoleon III. and the Nationality Principle
we add another, also British. In a work published in 1896, entitled "The Balkans,"

and Robert Browning's eulogium of France. This latter
occurs in Mr. Browning's poem entitled " Prince Hohenstiel Schwangau." Prince Hohenstiel stands for Louis Napoleon ; and, according to the author's dramatic method, the
eulogium is put into Napoleon's mouth. It is a noteworthy
fact that in the poem Napoleon is represented as giving a
justification, in part at least, of his life and purposes to a
woman whom we need not describe. Thus Mr. Browning,
whatever sympathies he entertained, as well as his wife, for
Napoleon, lashes in this cynical manner one of his faults.

Browning's eulogium of France is as follows : —

> " The people here,
> Earth presses to her heart, nor owns a pride
> Above her pride i' the race all flame and air
> And aspiration to the boundless Great,
> The incommeasurably Beautiful,—
> Whose very faulterings groundward come of flight
> Urged by a pinion all too passionate
> For heaven and what it holds of gloom and glow :
> Bravest of thinkers, bravest of the brave
> Doers, exalt in Science, rapturous
> In Art, the — more than all — magnetic race
> To fascinate their fellows, mould mankind." *

Mr. William Miller, referring to the State of Roumania (*i.e.*, Moldo-Wallachia) in 1848,
said, " The revolutionary leaders of 1848 had been inspired by the idea of national unity ;
and their cause had gained the ardent support of Napoleon III., with whom the doctrine
of nationalities was a passion."

* The entire poem, save the last few pages, consists of a dream from which the emperor awakes. He makes some sententious remarks to the effect that people often de-
ceive themselves, and adds a word respecting the Hohenzollern candidature to the Spanish throne, which had just appeared, and in the course of a few weeks was to destroy
perhaps his dynasty, certainly himself.

www.ingramcontent.com/pod-product-compliance
Lightning Source LLC
Chambersburg PA
CBHW031808090426
42739CB00008B/1215